Lofoten Islands Hiking Guide

Self-Guided Trails, Multi-Day Routes, Travel Planning & Arctic Photography Spots

KROSS TOKS

TABLE OF CONTENTS

INTRODUCTION

The Lofoten Islands are among the most spectacular hiking destinations in the world. Rising dramatically from the Norwegian Sea, this Arctic archipelago combines rugged mountain peaks, deep fjords, pristine beaches, colorful fishing villages, and ever-changing skies into a landscape that feels almost unreal. Whether you are standing atop a windswept summit overlooking turquoise bays or walking along a quiet coastal trail beneath the glow of the midnight sun, Lofoten offers experiences that remain etched in memory long after the journey ends.

What makes the Lofoten Islands particularly appealing is their remarkable accessibility. Despite their remote location above the Arctic Circle, visitors can reach world-class hiking trails within minutes of charming villages, comfortable accommodations, and reliable transportation networks. The region offers opportunities for every type of traveler—from first-time hikers seeking scenic day walks to experienced adventurers looking for challenging mountain ascents and multi-day trekking routes.

This guidebook was created to help you explore the Lofoten Islands with confidence, whether you are planning a short holiday or an extended hiking expedition. Rather than focusing solely on trail descriptions, it provides a complete framework for organizing a successful trip. Inside these pages, you will find practical travel advice, route-planning strategies, transportation information, accommodation options, safety guidance, seasonal considerations, photography recommendations, and detailed hiking insights tailored specifically to the unique conditions of Arctic Norway.

One of the greatest challenges visitors face is understanding how quickly conditions can change in the Lofoten Islands. Weather patterns are highly dynamic, daylight hours vary dramatically throughout the year, and many trails require careful preparation despite their relatively short distances. This book aims to simplify that process by presenting clear, reliable information that allows you to make informed decisions before and during your journey.

Photography enthusiasts will also discover a wealth of opportunities throughout the region. The combination of jagged mountains, mirror-like fjords, traditional fishing communities, northern lights displays, and the famous midnight sun creates some of the most photogenic scenery found anywhere in the Arctic. Dedicated sections throughout this guide highlight locations and techniques that can help both beginners and experienced photographers capture memorable images.

Beyond the landscapes themselves, the Lofoten Islands offer a rich cultural experience. Generations of fishing traditions, resilient coastal communities, and strong connections to the surrounding environment have shaped a distinctive local identity. Taking time to appreciate this heritage adds depth and meaning to any hiking adventure, transforming a simple outdoor excursion into a broader exploration of northern Norwegian life.

As you work through this guide, remember that successful hiking in Lofoten is not measured by the number of peaks climbed or kilometers covered. The true reward lies in experiencing the region safely, responsibly, and at a pace that allows you to fully appreciate its extraordinary beauty. Some days may be spent summiting famous viewpoints, while others may be dedicated to wandering quiet beaches, photographing dramatic weather, or simply enjoying the peaceful atmosphere of a remote Arctic village.

Whether your goal is to complete iconic summit hikes, embark on multi-day trekking routes, photograph the northern lights, or discover hidden corners away from the crowds, this guide is designed to help you plan and execute a rewarding adventure. The Lofoten Islands offer endless opportunities for exploration, and with thoughtful preparation, they can become one of the most unforgettable hiking destinations you will ever experience.

Welcome to the Lofoten Islands. Your Arctic adventure begins here.

CHAPTER 1: GETTING TO KNOW THE LOFOTEN ISLANDS

Geography And Natural Landscapes

The first thing that struck me when I arrived in the Lofoten Islands was how dramatically the landscape rose from the sea. Unlike many mountain regions where peaks gradually increase in elevation, Lofoten's mountains seem to emerge directly from the ocean. Sharp ridges, narrow valleys, deep fjords, and white-sand beaches exist side by side, creating one of the most visually impressive hiking destinations I have ever explored.

The Lofoten archipelago stretches across northern Norway above the Arctic Circle. Although the islands cover a relatively compact area, the variety of terrain is remarkable. In a single day, I could hike a mountain summit, walk along a coastal beach, and explore a fishing village without traveling long distances.

One practical advantage for hikers is the close proximity of trails to roads and communities. Many trailheads are easy to access, allowing visitors to maximize hiking time. Despite this accessibility, the scenery often feels remote and untouched. Understanding the geography of the islands helps when planning routes because weather, terrain, and travel times are heavily influenced by the mountainous landscape.

Climate And Seasonal Variations

Before visiting Lofoten, I assumed that being above the Arctic Circle would automatically mean extreme cold. While winters can certainly be harsh, I quickly learned that the surrounding ocean moderates temperatures more than many travelers expect. Conditions remain highly variable throughout the year, making seasonal planning essential.

Summer offers long daylight hours, with the midnight sun providing nearly continuous light. This creates excellent opportunities for hiking because I never felt rushed to finish a trail before darkness arrived. Temperatures are generally comfortable for outdoor activities, although rain and wind can still appear unexpectedly.

Autumn brings colorful landscapes and fewer visitors. I found this season ideal for those who prefer quieter trails and dramatic photography conditions. Winter transforms the islands into a snow-covered environment where northern lights become a major attraction. Spring offers a balance between increasing daylight and reduced visitor numbers.

One lesson I learned quickly was never to rely solely on weather forecasts from several days earlier. Conditions can change rapidly. Carrying waterproof layers and preparing for multiple weather scenarios is one of the most important habits any visitor can develop.

Culture, History, And Local Traditions

While many travelers come primarily for the scenery, I discovered that understanding the cultural history of Lofoten adds significant value to the hiking experience. For centuries, fishing has shaped life throughout the islands. The seasonal cod fisheries helped establish communities that continue to play an important role in the local economy today.

As I traveled between villages, I noticed traditional red fishing cabins known as rorbuer lining the waterfront. Many of these historic buildings have been preserved and converted into accommodations for visitors. Staying in one provided a deeper appreciation for the region's maritime heritage.

Local traditions emphasize resilience, community cooperation, and respect for nature. These values are reflected in how residents interact with the environment. Trails are generally well maintained, and visitors are encouraged to leave natural areas undisturbed.

I also found that small museums, cultural centers, and fishing villages offered valuable insights into how generations adapted to life in a rugged Arctic environment. Taking time to explore these cultural attractions creates a more complete understanding of the islands beyond their hiking opportunities.

Wildlife And Marine Ecosystems

One of the most rewarding aspects of hiking in Lofoten is the opportunity to observe wildlife in its natural habitat. Although large land mammals are relatively limited compared to some wilderness destinations, the marine ecosystem supports a rich variety of species.

During my visits, seabirds were among the most commonly encountered wildlife. Eagles, gulls, puffins, and other coastal birds can often be seen near cliffs and shorelines. Birdwatchers will find many opportunities throughout the islands, particularly during nesting seasons.

The surrounding waters are equally impressive. Whales, dolphins, seals, and various fish species inhabit the region. While marine wildlife sightings are never guaranteed, they contribute to the unique character of the islands.

Respecting wildlife is essential. I always maintained a safe distance, avoided disturbing nesting areas, and followed local guidelines. Responsible behavior not only protects animals but also ensures that future visitors can enjoy similar experiences.

The connection between land and sea is one of Lofoten's defining features. Understanding this relationship helps hikers appreciate how ecosystems, local communities, and outdoor recreation are interconnected.

Regions And Key Hiking Areas

As I explored different parts of the archipelago, I realized that each region offers its own distinct hiking experience. Knowing the characteristics of various areas helps travelers select routes that match their interests and abilities.

The southern islands are famous for dramatic peaks, picturesque fishing villages, and some of the most photographed landscapes in Norway. These areas often attract first-time visitors because they combine iconic viewpoints with relatively accessible trails.

Central Lofoten provides a mixture of coastal walks, mountain routes, and cultural attractions. I found this region particularly convenient because it offers a balance between hiking opportunities and visitor services.

Northern sections of the islands generally receive fewer visitors, creating a quieter atmosphere for those seeking solitude. The landscapes remain equally impressive, but the experience often feels more remote.

When planning hikes, I recommend considering travel times between regions. Although distances may appear short on a map, winding roads, bridges, and changing weather conditions can extend journey times. Building flexibility into an itinerary allows hikers to adapt and fully enjoy what each region has to offer.

By understanding the geography, climate, culture, wildlife, and regional differences of the Lofoten Islands, I was able to approach my hikes with greater confidence and appreciation. This foundation made every trail more meaningful and transformed the journey into far more than a simple outdoor adventure.

CHAPTER 2: PLANNING YOUR LOFOTEN HIKING ADVENTURE

Choosing The Best Time To Visit

One of the most important decisions I made when planning my trip to the Lofoten Islands was choosing the right season. The experience can vary dramatically depending on the time of year, so understanding what each season offers helps avoid disappointment and allows for better preparation.

For hiking, I found that late spring through early autumn provides the most favorable conditions. During these months, trails are generally free from snow, transportation services operate more frequently, and accommodations are easier to access. Summer is especially attractive because of the midnight sun, which provides nearly endless daylight for exploring.

However, I also noticed that summer attracts the largest number of visitors. Popular trails, parking areas, and villages can become crowded during peak travel periods. If I wanted a quieter experience, I would choose late May, early June, or September when conditions remain suitable for hiking but visitor numbers are lower.

Winter appeals to travelers seeking northern lights and snow-covered scenery, but it requires different skills and equipment. Many hiking routes become significantly more challenging under winter conditions. For most visitors focused primarily on hiking, the warmer months provide the best balance of accessibility, safety, and trail variety.

Setting Realistic Hiking Goals

Before arriving in Lofoten, I spent time evaluating my fitness level, hiking experience, and personal interests. This step proved extremely valuable because the islands offer a wide range of trails, from short scenic walks to demanding mountain ascents.

I learned that distance alone does not accurately reflect trail difficulty. Many Lofoten hikes involve steep climbs, uneven terrain, exposed sections, and rapidly changing weather. A route that appears short on paper may require considerable effort.

When planning my hikes, I divided potential routes into three categories: easy, moderate, and challenging. This approach allowed me to gradually build confidence while adjusting to local conditions. Starting with less demanding trails helped me understand the terrain before attempting more ambitious objectives.

I also considered non-hiking activities when setting goals. Photography, cultural exploration, village visits, and scenic drives added variety to my itinerary and prevented exhaustion. Trying to summit every famous peak within a limited timeframe can turn an enjoyable trip into a stressful experience.

The most satisfying travel plans are often those that leave room for flexibility. By prioritizing quality experiences rather than simply checking destinations off a list, I enjoyed the islands far more.

Budgeting For Your Trip

Norway is widely recognized as an expensive destination, and I quickly discovered that careful budgeting was essential. Fortunately, with proper planning, it is possible to manage costs without sacrificing the quality of the experience.

Accommodation usually represents one of the largest expenses. Prices vary significantly depending on location, season, and booking timing. I found that reserving accommodations well in advance often resulted in better rates and a wider selection of options.

Transportation costs should also be considered carefully. Flights, ferries, vehicle rentals, fuel, parking fees, and public transportation can add up quickly. Calculating these expenses before departure helped me avoid surprises.

Food is another major factor. Dining out regularly can become costly, so I often combined restaurant meals with groceries purchased from local supermarkets. Preparing simple breakfasts and trail lunches reduced daily expenses considerably.

I also created a small emergency fund for unexpected situations such as weather-related itinerary changes or additional transportation needs. This financial buffer provided peace of mind and allowed me to adapt when plans changed.

By tracking expected expenses in advance, I was able to focus on enjoying the journey rather than constantly worrying about costs.

Creating A Personalized Itinerary

When I first began researching the Lofoten Islands, I was tempted to visit every famous location. After further planning, I realized that a personalized itinerary based on my interests would create a far better experience.

The first step was identifying my primary goals. Some travelers focus on mountain hiking, while others prioritize photography, cultural attractions, wildlife observation, or coastal scenery. Understanding my priorities helped me allocate time more effectively.

I then grouped destinations by geographic region. This reduced unnecessary driving and allowed me to explore each area more thoroughly. Instead of constantly moving between distant locations, I could spend additional time enjoying trails and attractions nearby.

Weather flexibility became another essential component of my itinerary. Conditions in Lofoten can change rapidly, and maintaining backup plans proved extremely useful. On days when mountain routes were affected by poor weather, I substituted lower-elevation hikes, village visits, or photography excursions.

I also avoided scheduling every hour of every day. Allowing free time created opportunities for spontaneous discoveries, unexpected viewpoints, and local experiences that often became some of the most memorable parts of the trip.

A well-designed itinerary should serve as a guide rather than a rigid schedule. Flexibility often leads to a more enjoyable and less stressful adventure.

Understanding Local Travel Logistics

One lesson I learned quickly was that successful hiking in Lofoten depends heavily on understanding local transportation and logistics. While the islands are connected by roads, bridges, and tunnels, travel times can be longer than expected due to winding routes and changing conditions.

I carefully researched transportation options before arriving. Travelers can combine flights, ferries, buses, rental vehicles, and bicycles depending on their preferred travel style. Each option has advantages and limitations.

Vehicle rentals provide the greatest flexibility, especially for accessing multiple trailheads. However, parking availability can be limited at popular hiking locations during busy periods. Arriving early often helps avoid congestion.

Public transportation serves many communities, but schedules may not always align perfectly with hiking plans. Checking timetables in advance reduces the risk of delays or missed connections.

I also paid close attention to accommodation locations. Staying near planned hiking areas minimized daily travel and allowed me to spend more time on the trails. This simple decision improved both efficiency and overall enjoyment.

Understanding logistics before arrival eliminated many common travel frustrations. With transportation, accommodations, and route planning organized in advance, I could focus fully on exploring the extraordinary landscapes that make the Lofoten Islands such a remarkable hiking destination.

CHAPTER 3: ESSENTIAL GEAR AND PACKING STRATEGIES

Clothing For Arctic Conditions

One of the biggest mistakes I nearly made before visiting the Lofoten Islands was assuming that summer weather above the Arctic Circle would always be cold and miserable. The reality is more complex. During my hikes, I experienced sunshine, rain, wind, and sudden temperature shifts within the same day. Because of this, clothing selection became one of the most important factors affecting my comfort and safety.

I found that layering worked far better than relying on a single heavy jacket. My base layer was designed to manage moisture and keep my skin dry during uphill climbs. Over that, I wore an insulating layer that provided warmth when temperatures dropped. Finally, I carried a waterproof and windproof outer shell that protected me from rain and strong coastal winds.

Cotton clothing rarely performed well during outdoor activities because it retained moisture and dried slowly. Instead, I relied on technical fabrics that remained comfortable even when conditions changed unexpectedly.

A lightweight hat and gloves were also useful, even during warmer months. Strong winds at higher elevations often created temperatures that felt significantly cooler than those at sea level. Having these small items available prevented unnecessary discomfort and allowed me to stay on the trail longer.

The goal was not to pack excessive clothing but to carry versatile layers that could adapt to changing conditions throughout the day.

Footwear And Trail Equipment

The steep terrain of Lofoten quickly taught me that proper footwear should never be treated as an afterthought. Many trails involve loose rocks, muddy sections, wet surfaces, and uneven ground. A comfortable pair of hiking boots or trail shoes can make a significant difference in both safety and enjoyment.

Before my trip, I made sure my footwear was fully broken in. New boots may look appealing, but long hikes can quickly reveal pressure points and create painful blisters. I always recommend testing footwear on local hikes before traveling.

Good traction proved particularly important. Several popular routes included steep sections where reliable grip increased confidence and reduced the risk of slipping. Waterproof footwear was also valuable because many trails remained wet even after dry weather.

In addition to footwear, I carried trekking poles on longer routes. While not essential for every hike, they helped reduce strain during steep descents and provided additional balance on uneven terrain.

Other useful equipment included a comfortable daypack, reusable water bottles, sunglasses, sunscreen, and a compact sitting pad for breaks. These items may seem minor individually, but together they contributed greatly to overall comfort during long days outdoors.

Choosing reliable equipment allowed me to focus on the scenery rather than dealing with preventable problems on the trail.

Navigation And Safety Essentials

One lesson I learned early was that beautiful trails do not eliminate the need for navigation skills. While many popular hikes in Lofoten are well known, weather conditions can reduce visibility quickly, making navigation more challenging than expected.

I never relied exclusively on a single navigation method. Instead, I carried both digital and offline resources. Mobile applications were useful, but batteries can fail and signal coverage is not guaranteed everywhere. Downloading offline maps before hiking proved extremely valuable.

A power bank became one of the most useful items in my backpack. Continuous use of navigation apps, photography equipment, and communication devices can drain batteries faster than many travelers anticipate.

Safety equipment also deserves careful consideration. I carried a basic first-aid kit containing blister treatment, bandages, pain relief medication, and essential personal items. Even minor injuries can become frustrating if supplies are unavailable.

Emergency communication planning was another important habit. Before beginning longer hikes, I informed someone about my intended route and estimated return time. This simple precaution requires minimal effort but can be extremely valuable if unexpected situations arise.

Preparation is not about expecting problems. It is about ensuring that minor issues remain manageable and do not escalate into serious difficulties.

Photography Gear For Outdoor Adventures

Photography is one of the primary reasons many people visit the Lofoten Islands, and I quickly understood why. Nearly every trail offers dramatic mountain views, coastal scenery, colorful fishing villages, and unique Arctic lighting conditions.

When selecting photography equipment, I focused on balancing image quality with portability. Carrying excessive gear can reduce hiking enjoyment, especially on steep trails. I chose equipment that met my photography goals without adding unnecessary weight.

A weather-resistant camera proved particularly useful. Sudden rain showers are common, and having equipment capable of handling challenging conditions provided peace of mind. Protective covers for cameras and lenses were equally important.

Extra batteries became essential because cooler temperatures can reduce battery performance. I also carried additional memory cards to avoid running out of storage during long days in the field.

For those interested in landscape photography, a lightweight tripod can be valuable for sunrise, sunset, and northern lights photography. However, I carefully evaluated whether specific hikes justified carrying additional weight.

Photography in Lofoten is often less about technical perfection and more about being prepared when extraordinary conditions appear. Some of my favorite images resulted from unexpected moments that lasted only a few minutes.

Packing Efficiently For Multi-Day Treks

Packing for multi-day adventures requires a different approach than preparing for single-day hikes. Early in my planning process, I realized that every item carried over several days would influence my energy levels and overall comfort.

The most effective strategy was evaluating each item based on necessity and usefulness. If an object served only a limited purpose, I often left it behind. Lightweight, multi-functional equipment became my priority.

I organized gear into categories such as clothing, shelter, food, navigation, safety, and personal items. This system made packing more efficient and allowed me to quickly locate essential equipment when needed.

Waterproof storage bags were particularly valuable. Even if a backpack includes weather protection, additional waterproof organization helps keep critical items dry during prolonged rain.

Food planning also played an important role. I selected meals and snacks that provided high energy while remaining relatively lightweight. Carrying excessive food adds unnecessary weight, while insufficient nutrition can reduce performance on demanding trails.

Perhaps the most important lesson I learned was that successful packing is not about bringing everything that might be useful. It is about bringing the right items for the specific conditions expected during the trip. Thoughtful packing reduces physical strain, increases efficiency, and allows more energy to be devoted to enjoying the remarkable landscapes of the Lofoten Islands.

CHAPTER 4: TRANSPORTATION AND GETTING AROUND

Arriving By Air, Ferry, And Road

One of the first challenges I faced when planning my trip to the Lofoten Islands was understanding the various transportation options available. Although the islands are located above the Arctic Circle, reaching them is far easier than many travelers expect. What made the difference for me was selecting the arrival method that matched my schedule, budget, and travel goals.

Flying was the fastest option. Several airports serve the region, making it possible to arrive relatively quickly from other parts of Norway and Europe. For travelers with limited vacation time, flying allows more days to be spent hiking rather than traveling.

Ferries provide a different experience altogether. Arriving by sea offered me my first dramatic views of the mountains rising directly from the water. The approach created a memorable introduction to the islands and immediately highlighted the region's unique geography.

Driving into the area can also be rewarding, especially for travelers exploring northern Norway as part of a longer journey. Road travel allows flexibility and access to scenic viewpoints along the way. However, long driving distances should not be underestimated. Northern Norway covers vast areas, and travel times are often longer than maps initially suggest.

Choosing the right arrival method depends on individual priorities. Whether speed, scenery, flexibility, or budget is most important, understanding the available options helps create a smoother start to the adventure.

Renting Vehicles And Campervans

After researching various transportation methods, I found that renting a vehicle provided the greatest freedom for exploring the Lofoten Islands. Many hiking trailheads are located outside village centers, and having my own transportation allowed me to create a flexible daily schedule.

A standard rental car works well for most visitors because roads throughout the islands are generally in good condition. I rarely encountered situations that required specialized vehicles. The main advantage was the ability to reach trailheads early before parking areas became crowded.

Campervans have become increasingly popular among travelers seeking a combination of transportation and accommodation. I understood the appeal immediately.

Waking up near spectacular landscapes and having the flexibility to change plans based on weather conditions can greatly enhance the overall experience.

However, I also learned that responsible campervan travel is essential. Parking restrictions, camping regulations, and environmental considerations must be respected. Not every scenic location permits overnight stays, and understanding local rules helps avoid problems.

Fuel costs should also be included in trip planning. While distances within the islands are relatively manageable, frequent exploration can increase transportation expenses over time.

For hikers who value flexibility and independence, renting a vehicle remains one of the most effective ways to experience the region.

Using Public Transportation

Although many visitors choose rental vehicles, I discovered that public transportation can be a practical alternative, particularly for travelers seeking to reduce expenses or minimize environmental impact.

Buses connect many communities throughout the islands, making it possible to reach a surprising number of destinations without a private vehicle. With careful planning, I found that public transportation could support a rewarding hiking itinerary.

The key to success is understanding schedules before setting out. Bus services may operate less frequently than visitors from large cities are accustomed to. Missing a connection can significantly affect daily plans, especially in remote areas.

I made it a habit to review schedules in advance and allow extra time for transfers. This approach reduced stress and helped me avoid unnecessary delays. Having backup options also proved useful when weather conditions affected travel plans.

One advantage of public transportation is that it allows hikers to complete point-to-point routes without returning to the original starting location. In some cases, this creates opportunities for more varied and efficient hiking experiences.

While public transportation requires greater planning than driving, it remains a viable option for travelers willing to organize their itineraries carefully.

Navigating Between Islands

One aspect of Lofoten that surprised me was how seamlessly many of the islands are connected. Before arriving, I imagined a series of isolated landmasses requiring constant ferry travel. In reality, an impressive network of bridges, tunnels, and roads links much of the archipelago.

This infrastructure makes exploration remarkably convenient. Traveling between major hiking areas often requires less effort than visitors initially expect. Nevertheless, journey times should still be planned carefully because roads frequently follow winding coastal routes rather than direct paths.

I learned that weather can occasionally influence transportation conditions. Strong winds, heavy rain, and winter storms may affect travel schedules and road safety. Monitoring forecasts became a regular part of my daily planning routine.

When moving between islands, I also allowed time for scenic stops. Some of the most memorable viewpoints were found along the roads themselves rather than at designated hiking destinations. Rushing from one trailhead to another would have caused me to miss many remarkable landscapes.

Understanding the regional road network improved both efficiency and enjoyment. Rather than viewing transportation simply as a means of reaching hikes, I began treating the journeys themselves as part of the overall adventure.

Sustainable Travel Options

As tourism continues to grow throughout the Lofoten Islands, I became increasingly aware of the importance of making responsible transportation choices. The natural beauty that attracts visitors is also one of the region's most valuable resources, and preserving it requires thoughtful travel practices.

Whenever possible, I combined activities within the same geographic area rather than making unnecessary long-distance trips. This reduced fuel consumption while allowing me to explore destinations more thoroughly.

Walking and cycling also offered rewarding alternatives for shorter distances. Many communities are compact enough to explore comfortably on foot, providing opportunities to experience local culture at a slower pace.

Carpooling can further reduce environmental impact, especially for travelers exploring similar hiking destinations.

Sharing transportation not only lowers costs but also decreases congestion at popular trailheads and parking areas.

I also made an effort to support businesses that demonstrated environmental responsibility. Sustainable tourism depends on cooperation between visitors, local communities, and service providers.

By approaching transportation with environmental awareness, I found that my travel experience became more meaningful. Responsible choices helped protect the landscapes I came to admire while ensuring that future visitors would have the opportunity to enjoy the same extraordinary scenery that makes the Lofoten Islands one of the world's premier hiking destinations.

CHAPTER 5: SAFETY, WEATHER, AND TRAIL PREPAREDNESS

Understanding Rapid Weather Changes

One of the first lessons I learned while hiking in the Lofoten Islands was that weather can change much faster than many visitors expect. A clear morning can quickly turn into a windy afternoon, followed by rain and reduced visibility before the day ends. Because of this, I never relied solely on the weather conditions I observed when leaving my accommodation.

I made it a habit to check forecasts regularly, but I also understood that forecasts are only part of the preparation process. Conditions in mountainous coastal environments can shift rapidly, especially at higher elevations. The weather near sea level may appear calm while mountain ridges experience strong winds and significantly colder temperatures.

To stay prepared, I always carried waterproof outer layers, extra clothing, and basic emergency supplies even when the forecast looked favorable. There were several occasions when this extra preparation prevented a comfortable hike from becoming an unpleasant experience.

I also learned to recognize warning signs such as darkening clouds, increasing wind speeds, and sudden temperature drops. These indicators often helped me make good decisions before conditions deteriorated further.

The safest approach is to respect the weather at all times. If conditions become unsafe, turning back is not a failure. In my experience, protecting personal safety is always more important than reaching a summit.

Assessing Trail Difficulty Levels

Before hiking in Lofoten, I made the mistake of assuming that shorter trails would automatically be easier. After completing several routes, I quickly realized that distance alone tells only part of the story.

Many of the islands' most famous hikes involve steep ascents, rocky terrain, exposed ridges, and uneven surfaces. Some trails gain significant elevation over relatively short distances. As a result, a route lasting only a few hours can still be physically demanding.

When evaluating trail difficulty, I considered several factors beyond distance. Elevation gain, trail surface, weather exposure, technical sections, and available daylight all influenced the overall challenge. Reviewing these details before starting a hike allowed me to choose routes that matched my fitness level and experience.

I also avoided comparing myself with other hikers. Every person has different strengths, limitations, and comfort levels. A route that feels manageable for one visitor may be extremely demanding for another.

Building experience gradually proved to be one of the smartest decisions I made. Starting with easier hikes allowed me to understand local trail conditions before attempting more challenging routes. This approach increased both safety and enjoyment throughout my trip.

Emergency Planning And Communication

Although most hikes in Lofoten are completed without incident, I always believed that preparation for unexpected situations is essential. A minor injury, navigation error, or sudden weather change can become more serious if proper planning is neglected.

Before each hike, I informed someone about my planned route and expected return time. This simple habit required very little effort but provided an important safety measure. If something unexpected occurred, another person would know where to begin looking.

I also carried a fully charged mobile phone and a backup power source. Even though phone coverage is available in many areas, I never assumed it would be reliable everywhere. Downloading offline maps before starting a hike ensured that I could still navigate if network access became unavailable.

A compact first-aid kit remained in my backpack at all times. Blister treatment, bandages, antiseptic supplies, and personal medications were among the most useful items I carried.

Perhaps the most valuable part of emergency planning was maintaining good judgment. Many accidents occur when hikers continue despite worsening conditions or physical exhaustion. Knowing when to stop, rest, or return can prevent minor problems from becoming emergencies.

Wildlife Awareness And Environmental Risks

While the Lofoten Islands are not known for dangerous wildlife encounters, understanding the local environment remains an important aspect of trail safety. During my hikes, I encountered seabirds, coastal wildlife, and various marine species, all of which contributed to the unique character of the region.

The greatest environmental risks often came not from animals but from the landscape itself. Wet rocks, slippery boardwalks, muddy sections, and steep slopes required constant attention. After rainfall, many trails became considerably more challenging.

Cliff edges deserve particular respect. Some viewpoints offer spectacular scenery, but strong winds and loose surfaces can create dangerous conditions. I always maintained a safe distance from exposed edges, especially during periods of poor weather.

Another factor I considered was cold exposure. Even during summer, prolonged wind and rain can lower body temperature surprisingly quickly. Carrying extra layers and remaining dry helped reduce this risk significantly.

By focusing on environmental awareness rather than simply reaching destinations, I found that my hikes became both safer and more enjoyable.

Responsible Hiking Practices

One of the most rewarding aspects of visiting the Lofoten Islands was experiencing landscapes that remain remarkably beautiful and largely unspoiled. Preserving these environments requires responsible behavior from every visitor.

I always stayed on established trails whenever possible. This practice protects fragile vegetation and reduces erosion in sensitive areas. Straying from designated routes may seem harmless, but repeated impacts can damage ecosystems over time.

Waste management was another priority. Everything I brought onto a trail left with me, including food packaging and biodegradable items. Maintaining clean hiking areas helps preserve the natural experience for future visitors.

Respect for local communities also played an important role. Many trails pass near farms, fishing villages, and privately owned land. Following local guidelines and respecting property boundaries helps maintain positive relationships between residents and visitors.

Finally, I learned that responsible hiking includes respecting my own limits. Proper preparation, realistic expectations, and sound decision-making contribute to both personal safety and environmental protection.

The Lofoten Islands offer extraordinary hiking opportunities, but those opportunities come with responsibilities. By preparing carefully, respecting the environment, and prioritizing safety, I was able to enjoy the region's remarkable landscapes while helping ensure they remain accessible and protected for future generations of hikers.

CHAPTER 6: BEST SELF-GUIDED DAY HIKES

Beginner-Friendly Coastal Trails

When I first arrived in the Lofoten Islands, I wanted to ease into the hiking experience rather than immediately tackling steep mountain routes. Fortunately, the region offers several coastal trails that are ideal for beginners while still delivering the dramatic scenery that makes Lofoten famous.

What impressed me most about these coastal walks was the balance between accessibility and beauty. Many routes follow shorelines, gentle hills, and open landscapes where navigation is straightforward. These trails allowed me to become familiar with local weather patterns, trail conditions, and terrain without excessive physical strain.

I found that coastal hikes were particularly rewarding during early mornings and evenings when the light created stunning reflections across the water. The slower pace also provided more opportunities to appreciate local wildlife, fishing villages, and ocean views.

For travelers new to hiking or those seeking a relaxed outdoor experience, coastal routes offer an excellent introduction to the islands. They require less technical ability while still providing memorable scenery and numerous photography opportunities.

Starting with beginner-friendly hikes helped me build confidence and establish a strong foundation for more challenging adventures later in the trip.

Moderate Mountain Ascents

After completing several easier walks, I felt ready to explore some of Lofoten's moderate mountain trails. These hikes provided a satisfying balance between physical challenge and accessibility, making them suitable for travelers with basic hiking experience and reasonable fitness levels.

One aspect I appreciated was how quickly the scenery changed as elevation increased. Within a relatively short period, I could move from sea level to elevated viewpoints overlooking fjords, beaches, and mountain ridges. The rewards often arrived long before reaching the summit.

Moderate ascents typically require careful pacing rather than advanced technical skills. I learned to maintain a steady rhythm, conserve energy, and take regular breaks when necessary. This approach made the climbs more enjoyable and allowed me to appreciate the surrounding landscapes.

Weather awareness remained important. Conditions at higher elevations often differed significantly from those at the trailhead. Carrying additional layers and monitoring forecasts helped me stay comfortable throughout the hikes.

For many visitors, moderate mountain routes represent the ideal balance between effort and reward. They provide spectacular viewpoints without demanding extensive mountaineering experience.

Scenic Ridge Walks

Some of my most memorable experiences in Lofoten came from hiking along scenic ridges. These routes offered uninterrupted views in multiple directions and created a strong sense of immersion within the surrounding landscape.

Walking along a ridge feels different from hiking through forests or valleys. With open views extending across mountains, islands, beaches, and the sea, every step reveals a new perspective. On clear days, visibility can stretch remarkably far, creating some of the most rewarding hiking experiences in the region.

However, ridge hikes also require greater attention to weather and personal comfort. Wind exposure is often more significant than on lower trails. I always carried protective clothing and paid close attention to changing conditions.

Another lesson I learned was the importance of pacing. The temptation to stop frequently for photographs can make progress slower than expected. Building extra time into the schedule allowed me to enjoy viewpoints without feeling rushed.

Scenic ridge walks are ideal for hikers who enjoy panoramic views and immersive landscapes. They often deliver some of the most iconic scenery that travelers associate with the Lofoten Islands.

Family-Friendly Hiking Routes

Not every hiking experience needs to involve steep climbs or long distances. During my travels, I discovered several routes that are well suited to families, casual walkers, and visitors seeking enjoyable outdoor experiences without significant physical demands.

Family-friendly trails often feature shorter distances, manageable terrain, and easy access from nearby communities. These routes provide opportunities to experience Lofoten's natural beauty while accommodating a wider range of ages and abilities.

I particularly appreciated how these hikes encouraged a slower pace. Instead of focusing solely on reaching a summit, I spent more time observing wildlife, exploring beaches, and enjoying the surrounding scenery. This relaxed approach often revealed details that might otherwise have been overlooked.

For families traveling with children, preparation remains important. Bringing extra clothing, snacks, water, and entertainment for breaks can make the experience more enjoyable for everyone involved.

These routes demonstrate that memorable hiking experiences are not defined by difficulty. Some of the most rewarding moments occur on simple trails where the emphasis is placed on exploration, learning, and spending time outdoors together.

Hidden Gems Away From Crowds

While many famous trails deserve their popularity, some of my favorite experiences occurred on lesser-known routes away from the busiest visitor areas. Exploring these hidden gems allowed me to experience a quieter side of the Lofoten Islands.

These less-visited trails often provided a stronger sense of solitude and connection with nature. On several occasions, I spent hours hiking without encountering large groups of people. The peaceful atmosphere enhanced both the hiking experience and my appreciation for the landscape.

Finding hidden gems requires research and flexibility. Local recommendations, detailed maps, and conversations with residents often revealed excellent alternatives to more crowded destinations. I discovered that many lesser-known trails offered scenery equal to that of famous viewpoints.

However, quieter routes sometimes come with fewer facilities and less obvious trail markings. Additional preparation, navigation awareness, and self-reliance become more important when venturing beyond the most popular areas.

One of the greatest advantages of exploring hidden locations is the opportunity to experience the islands at a more personal pace. Without crowds competing for viewpoints or parking spaces, I could fully absorb the surroundings and enjoy the sense of discovery that makes hiking so rewarding.

These hidden gems reminded me that the true value of a hiking adventure is not always found at the most famous destinations. Sometimes the most memorable experiences occur in places that receive far less attention but offer equally remarkable beauty.

CHAPTER 7: ICONIC SUMMITS AND VIEWPOINT HIKES

Reinebringen And Surrounding Peaks

When people think about hiking in the Lofoten Islands, one summit appears repeatedly in photographs, travel articles, and conversations among outdoor enthusiasts. Reinebringen is widely regarded as one of the most iconic viewpoints in the region, and after completing the hike myself, I understood exactly why.

The route is known for its steep ascent, but modern stone steps have improved safety and reduced erosion. Even so, I quickly realized that this is not simply a casual walk. The climb demands steady effort, particularly during busy periods when hikers may need to share narrow sections of the trail.

Upon reaching the viewpoint, I was rewarded with one of the most remarkable panoramas I had ever seen. The fishing village below, the surrounding fjords, and the sharp mountain peaks created a landscape that seemed almost unreal.

One practical lesson I learned was to start early whenever possible. Popular trails attract significant visitor numbers, especially during the summer season. Early departures often provide quieter conditions and better opportunities for photography.

The surrounding peaks also deserve attention. While Reinebringen receives much of the spotlight, nearby mountains offer equally impressive scenery and often provide a more peaceful hiking experience.

Ryten And Kvalvika Beach Route

Among all the hikes I completed in Lofoten, the route connecting Ryten and Kvalvika Beach remains one of the most balanced experiences. It combines mountain views, coastal scenery, and a rewarding sense of adventure without requiring advanced technical skills.

The hike begins with a gradual climb that eventually opens onto expansive viewpoints overlooking the coastline. As I gained elevation, the dramatic contrast between the mountains and the sea became increasingly impressive. The famous view toward Kvalvika Beach is particularly memorable because it captures many of the natural elements that define the Lofoten landscape.

What makes this route especially appealing is the opportunity to combine different environments within a single outing. After enjoying the elevated viewpoints, I descended toward the beach itself, where white sand and crashing waves created a completely different atmosphere.

I found this hike suitable for a wide range of hikers who possess moderate fitness levels. The terrain requires attention, but the route remains accessible to many visitors willing to invest the necessary effort.

For those seeking a classic Lofoten experience, few hikes combine mountains, coastline, and scenery as effectively as Ryten and Kvalvika Beach.

Festvågtind Scenic Climb

One of the most rewarding discoveries during my trip was Festvågtind. While it may not receive the same international attention as some of the region's most famous peaks, it offers exceptional views and a highly satisfying hiking experience.

The climb is relatively short, but the steep terrain ensures that it remains physically engaging. I appreciated the efficiency of the route because it delivered outstanding scenery without requiring an entire day.

As I approached higher elevations, views expanded across nearby bays, mountain ridges, and coastal communities. The summit itself provided a spectacular perspective over the surrounding landscape and offered excellent opportunities for photography.

I particularly enjoyed this hike during periods of stable weather when visibility extended far across the islands. The combination of ocean, mountains, and changing light created a constantly evolving scene.

One advantage of shorter summit hikes is the flexibility they provide. Festvågtind can often be combined with additional activities on the same day, making it a valuable option for travelers working within limited schedules.

The climb serves as a reminder that some of the most rewarding experiences are not necessarily found on the highest or most famous mountains.

Himmeltindan Mountain Adventure

For hikers seeking a greater challenge, Himmeltindan offers an experience that feels more adventurous and remote. I approached this route with respect because it demands both physical effort and careful preparation.

The trail gains significant elevation and traverses terrain that requires concentration and good judgment. Weather conditions become increasingly important as exposure increases, making proper planning essential.

What impressed me most about Himmeltindan was the sense of scale. From higher elevations, I could appreciate how interconnected the islands are. Fjords, villages, beaches, and distant peaks all combined into a vast Arctic panorama.

This hike reinforced the importance of pacing. Attempting to rush the ascent would have reduced both enjoyment and safety. By maintaining a steady rhythm and taking strategic breaks, I was able to fully appreciate the experience while managing energy effectively.

Himmeltindan may not be the ideal choice for first-time hikers, but for those with experience and preparation, it delivers a memorable mountain adventure and some of the finest viewpoints in the archipelago.

Completing the route left me with a strong sense of accomplishment and a deeper appreciation for the rugged beauty of the region.

Panoramic Arctic Viewpoints

While individual summits often receive the most attention, I discovered that the true magic of Lofoten lies in the collection of panoramic viewpoints scattered throughout the islands. Each offers a unique perspective on the Arctic landscape.

Some viewpoints reveal dramatic mountain ridges rising from the sea. Others overlook fishing villages, winding fjords, or remote beaches. No two locations felt exactly alike, and each provided a different understanding of the region's geography.

One strategy that improved my experience was timing visits carefully. Early mornings and late evenings often produced softer light, fewer crowds, and more dramatic photography conditions. During summer, the extended daylight hours created remarkable opportunities to explore viewpoints at unconventional times.

I also learned that weather plays a significant role in shaping the visual experience. Clear skies provide long-distance visibility, while clouds and changing conditions can add atmosphere and depth to photographs.

Perhaps the greatest lesson I gained from these panoramic viewpoints was the importance of slowing down. Rather than immediately taking photographs and moving on, I spent time simply observing the landscape. Those quiet moments often became the most memorable part of the journey.

The iconic summits and viewpoints of the Lofoten Islands are far more than hiking destinations. They are places where geography, weather, light, and perspective combine to create experiences that remain vivid long after the trip has ended.

CHAPTER 8: MULTI-DAY TREKKING ROUTES

Planning Extended Hiking Journeys

When I first considered spending multiple days hiking in the Lofoten Islands, I quickly realized that planning becomes significantly more important than for single-day hikes. Multi-day trekking requires a different mindset, where each decision influences not only the current day but also the overall flow of the journey.

I began by mapping out realistic daily distances based on terrain, elevation, and expected weather conditions. In Lofoten, even moderate distances can feel demanding due to steep climbs and unpredictable surfaces. I learned not to rely solely on kilometers when estimating effort.

Another important step was identifying logical start and end points that offered access to accommodation or camping areas. Unlike urban trekking environments, the islands require careful coordination between hiking routes and available services.

I also allowed flexibility within my plan. Weather changes frequently, and I found that rigid schedules often created unnecessary stress. Building buffer time into each day helped me adapt without feeling rushed or pressured.

Ultimately, I discovered that successful multi-day trekking depends less on covering distance and more on maintaining consistency, safety, and enjoyment throughout the entire journey.

Hut To Hut Trekking Opportunities

One of the most comfortable ways I experienced multi-day hiking in Lofoten was through hut-to-hut trekking. Staying in mountain cabins provided shelter, rest, and a sense of structure during longer routes.

These huts are typically simple but practical, offering essential protection from weather conditions that can change rapidly. After long hiking days, having a secure place to rest significantly improved my recovery and overall experience.

I appreciated the sense of community in these accommodations. Meeting other hikers from different backgrounds created opportunities to share trail experiences, compare routes, and exchange practical advice.

However, I quickly learned that hut availability can vary depending on the season. Planning and reservations are often necessary, especially during peak travel periods.

Spontaneous decisions are possible in some cases, but relying entirely on availability can be risky.

For me, hut-to-hut trekking provided a balanced combination of comfort and adventure, allowing me to explore longer routes without carrying excessive camping gear.

Wild Camping Considerations

At some point during my travels, I chose to explore wild camping as an alternative to structured accommodation. The experience offered a greater sense of freedom and a closer connection to nature, but it also required greater responsibility.

Selecting appropriate camping locations became one of the most important decisions each day. I focused on flat, stable ground that was away from sensitive vegetation and respected local guidelines regarding outdoor camping.

Weather conditions played a critical role in this decision-making process. Wind exposure in the Lofoten Islands can be strong, especially near coastal areas or elevated terrain. I learned to prioritize sheltered locations whenever possible.

Carrying lightweight but reliable equipment made a significant difference. A durable tent, waterproof protection, and proper insulation ensured that I remained comfortable even during challenging nights.

I also became more aware of environmental impact. Leaving no trace was not just a recommendation but a personal responsibility. Every campsite I used was left exactly as I found it.

Wild camping gave me a deeper appreciation of the landscape, but it also reinforced the importance of preparation and respect for the environment.

Route Linking And Logistics

One of the most complex aspects of multi-day trekking in Lofoten was understanding how individual trails connect across different regions. At first, I underestimated how important route linking would be for efficient travel.

I learned to study maps carefully and identify logical connections between hiking paths, roads, and villages. Some trails that appear close on a map may require additional travel time due to terrain or water crossings.

Transportation logistics also influenced my route decisions. In some cases, I planned hikes that ended near public transport points or accessible roads to simplify movement between stages.

Another important factor was food and supply planning. I identified locations where I could restock essential items and adjusted my route accordingly. This prevented unnecessary weight and ensured I always had sufficient supplies.

By understanding how different routes connect, I was able to design a smoother and more enjoyable trekking experience that reduced unnecessary backtracking and travel fatigue.

Managing Supplies On Longer Treks

Managing supplies over multiple days required careful balance between carrying enough essentials and avoiding excessive weight. Early in my planning, I realized that poor supply management can quickly affect energy levels and hiking performance.

Food selection was one of the most important considerations. I chose lightweight, high-energy meals that were easy to prepare and did not require complex cooking equipment. Snacks played a crucial role in maintaining stamina during long hiking days.

Water availability varied depending on location, so I always researched refill points in advance. Carrying a reliable water filtration method also provided flexibility in areas where natural sources were available.

Clothing management required similar attention. I packed only what was necessary for changing weather conditions, focusing on versatile layers rather than multiple redundant items.

I also monitored energy consumption closely. Multi-day hiking places consistent demand on the body, and proper nutrition and hydration became essential for maintaining performance.

Through experience, I learned that successful supply management is not about carrying everything possible, but about carrying only what is truly needed while maintaining flexibility for changing conditions.

Multi-day trekking in the Lofoten Islands taught me that preparation, adaptability, and simplicity are the foundations of a successful journey. When these elements are balanced correctly, extended hikes become not only achievable but deeply rewarding experiences that reveal the full character of the Arctic landscape.

CHAPTER 9: ACCOMMODATION AND CAMPING OPTIONS

Traditional Rorbu Stays

One of the most memorable parts of my time in the Lofoten Islands was staying in traditional rorbu cabins. These former fishing huts, often built on stilts above the water, gave me a direct connection to the region's maritime heritage while providing a comfortable base for hiking.

Inside, I found a balance between simplicity and practicality. Most rorbu accommodations offer essential amenities such as a warm sleeping area, kitchen facilities, and heating, which made them especially valuable after long days on the trail. Waking up to views of the fjords or fishing villages created a calm atmosphere that enhanced my overall experience.

Location played a major role in choosing where to stay. I learned that staying closer to hiking areas reduced travel time and allowed me to start early in the morning, which is particularly important during busy seasons. However, popular locations tend to book quickly, so advance planning became essential.

What I appreciated most about rorbu stays was the combination of comfort and cultural immersion. It felt like I was experiencing not just a place to sleep, but a living part of Lofoten's history.

Mountain Cabins And Huts

During longer hiking routes, mountain cabins and huts provided essential shelter and structure. These accommodations are more basic than rorbu cabins but are perfectly suited for multi-day trekking conditions.

I quickly learned to value the simplicity of these huts. After a demanding day of hiking, having a dry and secure place to rest made a significant difference in recovery. Even without luxury amenities, the protection they offered from wind, rain, and cold conditions was invaluable.

Many mountain huts are strategically located along established hiking routes, making them convenient stopping points for extended journeys. However, availability can vary depending on the season, so I always checked in advance when possible.

Another important aspect was sharing space with other hikers. These communal environments often led to interesting conversations and shared advice about trail conditions, weather updates, and route recommendations.

Staying in mountain huts reinforced my understanding that comfort in remote areas is not about luxury but about safety, rest, and practicality.

Campsites And Facilities

Camping provided me with one of the most flexible accommodation options in the Lofoten Islands. Official campsites are located throughout the region and often offer basic but reliable facilities such as toilets, cooking areas, and freshwater access.

I found campsites particularly useful when I wanted to stay close to specific hiking areas without committing to fixed accommodation schedules. This flexibility allowed me to adjust my plans based on weather conditions and personal energy levels.

One thing I noticed was the importance of arriving early during peak seasons. Popular campsites can fill quickly, especially those located near well-known hiking routes. Planning ahead or having alternative locations in mind helped avoid unnecessary stress.

Facilities varied from place to place, but even the simplest campsites provided a safe and designated area for overnight stays. This structure made camping more organized and reduced environmental impact compared to unregulated setups.

For me, campsites offered a practical balance between affordability, accessibility, and proximity to nature.

Wild Camping Regulations

While wild camping is part of Norway's outdoor culture, I quickly realized that it comes with clear expectations and responsibilities. Understanding and respecting these guidelines was essential for a safe and responsible experience.

I made sure to choose locations that were away from private property, cultivated land, and environmentally sensitive areas. Respecting these boundaries is not only a legal requirement in many cases but also a matter of respecting local communities and ecosystems.

Another important consideration was distance from roads and buildings. I always ensured that my camping spot was sufficiently remote to avoid disturbing residents or impacting farmland.

Environmental awareness was central to my approach. I avoided leaving any trace of my stay and took care not to damage vegetation or disturb wildlife. Even small actions can have long-term effects in fragile Arctic environments.

Weather also influenced my decisions significantly. Strong winds and sudden rain made location choice critical, and I learned to prioritize safety and shelter over scenic views when necessary.

Wild camping gave me freedom, but it also required discipline, awareness, and respect for both nature and local regulations.

Booking Strategies And Seasonal Demand

One of the most important lessons I learned about accommodation in Lofoten is that timing matters significantly. Demand fluctuates throughout the year, and popular locations can become fully booked well in advance.

During peak summer months, I found that early reservations provided the best selection and pricing options. Waiting too long often meant limited availability or longer travel distances to hiking areas.

I also learned to align accommodation choices with my hiking itinerary. Staying strategically within different regions of the islands reduced unnecessary travel time and made daily planning more efficient.

Flexibility remained important even after booking. Weather conditions or trail closures occasionally required adjustments, so I always preferred accommodations with reasonable cancellation policies when possible.

Understanding seasonal patterns helped me avoid unnecessary stress. Off-peak periods offered more availability and a quieter atmosphere, while peak seasons required more structured planning.

By combining early booking, strategic location selection, and flexible planning, I was able to create a stable base for exploring the Lofoten Islands while still maintaining freedom to adapt my hiking experience.

Accommodation choices in Lofoten are not just about where to sleep. They directly influence how efficiently and comfortably I was able to experience the landscapes, and careful planning significantly improved the overall quality of my journey.

CHAPTER 10: ARCTIC PHOTOGRAPHY AND SCENIC LOCATIONS

Capturing Mountain Landscapes

When I first arrived in the Lofoten Islands, I quickly realized that photography here is not just an activity but a natural part of the hiking experience. The dramatic combination of jagged peaks, fjords, and open sea created constant opportunities for composition, often without needing to search for them.

I focused on learning how to work with changing light rather than trying to control it. In the Arctic environment, conditions shift quickly, and a single location can look completely different within minutes. This taught me to be patient and observant rather than rushing from one viewpoint to another.

For mountain landscapes, I found that elevation played a major role in composition. Higher vantage points revealed layers of terrain that are not visible from lower trails. I often paused during ascents not just to rest, but to observe how the landscape unfolded as I climbed.

Weather also became an important creative element. Clouds, mist, and rain often added depth and atmosphere rather than reducing image quality. I learned to embrace imperfect conditions instead of waiting only for clear skies.

Photographing Coastal Villages

The coastal villages in Lofoten offered a completely different photographic experience compared to mountain trails. Instead of vast open landscapes, I focused on details such as colorful rorbu cabins, fishing boats, harbors, and daily life along the shoreline.

I discovered that timing was essential when photographing these areas. Early mornings often provided calm water reflections and soft light, while evenings added warm tones across the buildings and surrounding mountains. Midday light was less favorable, so I used that time for hiking instead of photography.

I also paid attention to perspective. Small changes in position could significantly alter the composition, especially in compact villages where elements are closely arranged. Walking slowly and observing angles helped me find more meaningful shots.

Another important aspect was respecting local life. Many of these villages are active communities, not just tourist locations. I made sure to photograph respectfully without disrupting daily activities or invading private spaces.

These coastal scenes gave me a deeper appreciation for how human life and natural landscapes coexist in the region.

Midnight Sun Photography Techniques

Experiencing the midnight sun in Lofoten was one of the most unusual and rewarding aspects of my journey. The extended daylight created unique opportunities where time of day felt less restrictive, allowing me to explore photography in a more flexible way.

I noticed that the quality of light during late evening hours was particularly soft and warm. Even when the sun was low on the horizon at unusual times, it produced long shadows and rich color tones that enhanced landscape images.

One adjustment I had to make was managing my own schedule. Without a natural sunset to signal the end of the day, I sometimes continued photographing much longer than expected. I learned to balance exploration with rest to maintain energy for hiking.

Camera settings also required adaptation. The constant light conditions meant I could shoot continuously without worrying about darkness, but changing exposure levels became important as light intensity shifted.

The midnight sun created a sense of timelessness that influenced not only my photography but also my overall perception of the environment.

Northern Lights Photography Basics

Although I visited during a period when the northern lights were not always visible, I still prepared for the possibility and learned the essential principles of capturing them. This preparation enhanced my understanding of low-light photography even when the aurora did not appear.

I learned that patience is critical. Northern lights are unpredictable, and successful photography depends on being in the right location at the right time under suitable conditions. Monitoring forecasts and staying in areas with low light pollution increased my chances.

A stable tripod became essential for long exposure shots. Without it, capturing sharp images in low light would have been nearly impossible. I also practiced adjusting camera settings in advance so I could react quickly if the aurora appeared.

Cold conditions required additional preparation. Batteries drained faster in low temperatures, so I kept spares close to my body to preserve power.

Even when the northern lights were not visible, the experience of waiting under Arctic skies created a sense of anticipation that made each night outdoors memorable.

Best Sunrise And Sunset Locations

Some of my most rewarding photography moments in Lofoten came from carefully choosing sunrise and sunset locations. The unique geography of the islands creates countless opportunities for dramatic lighting conditions.

I learned that elevation and direction matter significantly. Mountain viewpoints facing open horizons often provided the most striking light during sunrise and sunset periods. Coastal areas, on the other hand, offered reflections and foreground elements that enhanced composition.

Planning ahead became an important part of my routine. I often visited potential locations during daylight hours to understand access routes and composition possibilities before returning during optimal lighting conditions.

Weather added another layer of unpredictability. Clouds sometimes enhanced sunsets with dramatic color shifts, while clear skies produced more subtle tones. I learned not to dismiss a location based solely on weather forecasts.

One of my key lessons was that the best results often came from staying longer than planned. Light conditions can change rapidly, and some of the most impressive images appeared after the expected peak moments.

These sunrise and sunset experiences reminded me that photography in Lofoten is not about chasing perfection but about being present when natural light and landscape align in unexpected ways.

CHAPTER 11: FOOD, RESUPPLY, AND LOCAL EXPERIENCES

Grocery Stores And Resupply Points

During my time hiking in the Lofoten Islands, I quickly realized that managing food supplies is an essential part of trip planning. Unlike urban destinations, access to stores becomes more limited once you move between smaller villages or begin longer hiking routes.

I made it a habit to identify grocery stores in advance before setting out on each section of my journey. Larger towns offered more variety, while smaller communities had limited but sufficient selections for basic needs. Planning resupply points helped me avoid carrying excessive weight while ensuring I never ran short of essentials.

One thing I learned was to think strategically about timing. I often restocked food before starting longer hikes rather than waiting until supplies were low. This prevented unnecessary stress and allowed me to focus fully on the trail.

Simple, high-energy foods became my priority. Items that were easy to carry, quick to prepare, and calorie-dense worked best for long hiking days. I avoided overcomplicating meals, especially when staying in remote areas where cooking facilities were limited.

Resupply planning gave me greater independence on the trail and allowed me to adjust my itinerary more freely when needed.

Traditional Norwegian Cuisine

Exploring local food became an important part of my experience in Lofoten. After long hiking days, I often looked forward to trying traditional Norwegian dishes that reflected the region's coastal culture and fishing heritage.

Fish-based meals were especially common, and I noticed how fresh local ingredients influenced even simple dishes. Many meals were prepared in a way that highlighted natural flavors rather than heavy seasoning or complex preparation.

I also found that portion sizes were often generous, which was helpful after physically demanding hikes. Eating locally provided not only nutrition but also a deeper connection to the environment I was exploring.

One observation I made was that food culture in Lofoten is closely tied to the sea. This connection appears in both traditional recipes and modern dining options.

Understanding this relationship added more meaning to every meal I experienced.

Trying local cuisine became more than just eating. It became part of understanding how communities have adapted to life in a challenging Arctic environment.

Dining In Remote Areas

While larger villages offered restaurants and cafes, I learned that dining options become more limited as you move into remote areas of the Lofoten Islands. This required adjusting expectations and planning accordingly.

I often combined restaurant meals with self-prepared food. After completing difficult hikes, I appreciated having the option to enjoy a warm meal in a local establishment. However, I never relied solely on restaurants due to their limited availability in some areas.

One thing I noticed was that remote dining experiences tend to be simple but satisfying. The focus is often on fresh ingredients and practical meals rather than elaborate menus. This simplicity matched the overall atmosphere of the region.

I also learned to be flexible with timing. Some establishments operate on seasonal schedules or reduced hours, especially in less populated areas. Checking opening times in advance became part of my routine planning process.

Dining in remote areas reminded me that simplicity often enhances the experience rather than limiting it.

Water Sources And Trail Nutrition

Hydration and nutrition were critical components of my hiking experience in the Lofoten Islands. Even though water sources are available in many areas, I never assumed access without verifying conditions in advance.

I carried sufficient water for each hike but also researched potential refill points along the route. In some locations, natural water sources were available, but I always treated water carefully before consumption to ensure safety.

Trail nutrition played an equally important role. I learned to choose foods that provided steady energy rather than short bursts. Snacks such as nuts, dried foods, and energy bars helped maintain stamina during long ascents.

I also paid attention to timing. Eating small amounts regularly during hikes proved more effective than waiting until I felt fatigued. This approach helped maintain consistent energy levels throughout the day.

Proper hydration and nutrition allowed me to hike longer distances comfortably and recover more quickly after demanding routes.

Cultural Experiences Beyond Hiking

While hiking was the main focus of my trip, I discovered that some of the most memorable experiences in Lofoten came from moments outside the trails. Taking time to engage with local culture added depth to my journey.

I visited small museums, fishing villages, and cultural sites that helped me understand how life in the region has evolved over time. These experiences provided context for the landscapes I was exploring and the communities living within them.

I also appreciated simple interactions with local residents. Conversations about weather, fishing traditions, and daily life offered insights that could not be found in guidebooks. These exchanges made the trip feel more personal and meaningful.

One important realization I had was that cultural experiences and outdoor exploration are closely connected in Lofoten. Understanding local life enhanced my appreciation of the landscapes and made each hike feel more significant.

By combining hiking with cultural exploration, I gained a more complete understanding of the region. The experience became not just about reaching destinations but about connecting with the environment and the people who call it home.

CHAPTER 12: SUSTAINABLE AND RESPONSIBLE EXPLORATION

Leave No Trace Principles

From my first hike in the Lofoten Islands, I became aware that preserving the environment is not an abstract idea but a daily responsibility. The landscapes are striking, yet also fragile, and every visitor has an impact whether they realize it or not.

I made it a habit to follow leave no trace principles strictly on every hike. This meant carrying out everything I brought in, including small items that are often overlooked. Even biodegradable waste was treated with caution because decomposition behaves differently in cold, coastal environments.

I also avoided disturbing natural features such as rocks, vegetation, and shoreline formations. Staying on established paths whenever possible helped reduce erosion and protected areas that are sensitive to repeated foot traffic.

One of the most important lessons I learned was that small actions accumulate. A single shortcut off-trail or discarded item may seem insignificant, but multiplied by thousands of visitors, the impact becomes serious.

Practicing leave no trace principles changed the way I moved through the landscape. I became more deliberate, more observant, and more respectful of the environment surrounding me.

Protecting Fragile Arctic Environments

The Arctic environment in Lofoten is both beautiful and delicate. During my hikes, I noticed how quickly vegetation can be affected by repeated foot traffic and how slow natural recovery can be in colder climates.

I made a conscious effort to minimize my impact, especially in areas with soft ground, moss, and coastal vegetation. These surfaces are easily damaged and can take years to recover if disturbed.

Weather also plays a role in environmental sensitivity. Wet conditions make trails more vulnerable to erosion, so I adjusted my route choices when necessary to avoid contributing to unnecessary wear.

I learned that respecting the environment sometimes means choosing not to hike certain areas when conditions are poor. This decision prioritizes long-term preservation over short-term exploration.

Understanding the fragility of Arctic ecosystems gave me a deeper appreciation for the responsibility that comes with visiting such regions. It also influenced how I planned and executed each hike.

Respecting Local Communities

While the natural environment is a major attraction, I quickly realized that local communities are equally important to the character of the Lofoten Islands. Many hiking routes pass near villages, private land, and working fishing areas.

I made sure to respect private property boundaries and follow local guidelines wherever I traveled. This included being mindful of noise levels, parking locations, and access restrictions.

One thing I noticed was that local residents maintain a strong connection to their environment and traditions. This influenced how I behaved as a visitor. I aimed to move through the area with awareness rather than treating it as an isolated outdoor playground.

I also found that showing respect often led to more positive interactions. Simple gestures such as greeting locals, following posted signs, and asking permission when necessary created a more meaningful travel experience.

Respecting communities was not only about following rules but also about understanding that people live and work in the same landscapes that visitors come to admire.

Minimizing Travel Impact

As I spent more time exploring the Lofoten Islands, I began to think more carefully about the broader impact of my travel decisions. Transportation, accommodation, and daily activities all contribute to environmental pressure in different ways.

I made small adjustments to reduce unnecessary movement between locations. Instead of constantly changing base areas, I grouped hikes within the same region whenever possible. This reduced fuel consumption and allowed me to explore areas more deeply.

I also considered transportation alternatives such as shared travel options and walking short distances instead of driving. These choices not only reduced environmental impact but also helped me experience the landscape more closely.

Energy use and resource consumption became part of my awareness as well. I tried to be mindful of water usage, electricity consumption, and general waste production during my stay.

Minimizing travel impact did not require major sacrifices. Instead, it involved consistent small decisions that collectively made my trip more responsible and sustainable.

Supporting Local Businesses

One of the most meaningful ways I contributed during my visit was by supporting local businesses. I realized that tourism has a direct influence on small communities in the Lofoten Islands, and choosing where to spend money matters.

I prioritized locally owned accommodations, food providers, and services whenever possible. This helped ensure that my spending directly supported the communities I was visiting rather than larger external operators.

I also noticed that local businesses often provide more authentic experiences. Whether it was accommodation in a fishing village or a small café near a hiking route, these places reflected the culture and character of the region more closely.

Supporting local enterprises also gave me a better understanding of daily life in the islands. Conversations with business owners often revealed insights about weather patterns, trail conditions, and cultural traditions that I would not have discovered otherwise.

Over time, I came to see responsible spending as part of responsible travel. My choices contributed not only to my own experience but also to the sustainability of the communities that make the Lofoten Islands such a unique hiking destination.

This chapter reinforced my belief that sustainable exploration is not a limitation but an enhancement. It deepens the connection between visitor, environment, and community, creating a more meaningful and lasting travel experience.

CHAPTER 13: FINAL PLANNING CHECKLIST AND PRACTICAL ADVICE

Pre Trip Preparation Essentials

Before setting off for the Lofoten Islands, I learned that thorough preparation is the foundation of a successful hiking experience. Even though the region is accessible and well known for outdoor tourism, I realized that conditions can still be demanding and unpredictable.

I began my preparation by reviewing my planned hiking routes in detail. This included understanding distance, elevation gain, terrain type, and estimated completion times. I avoided relying only on general descriptions and instead focused on practical details that would affect daily performance.

I also made sure my physical condition matched the demands of the terrain. While the hikes are not technical in a mountaineering sense, the combination of steep ascents and changing weather requires a reasonable level of fitness.

Packing was another critical step. I focused on essential items rather than excess gear, ensuring that everything I carried served a clear purpose. This approach reduced weight and made hiking more comfortable over long distances.

By preparing carefully in advance, I was able to start my journey with confidence and avoid unnecessary complications during the trip.

Essential Gear Final Review

Before beginning any hike, I always performed a final check of my equipment. This habit helped me identify missing items or unnecessary weight before it became a problem on the trail.

My essential gear included layered clothing suitable for changing weather, waterproof protection, and reliable footwear. I paid particular attention to ensuring everything was functional and in good condition.

Navigation tools were also part of my final review. I carried both digital and offline maps to ensure I could navigate even in areas with limited signal coverage. A fully charged power bank was included to support extended use of electronic devices.

Safety equipment such as a compact first aid kit, emergency supplies, and extra insulation layers was always double-checked. Even if not used frequently, these items provided reassurance in remote environments.

This final gear review became a habit that significantly reduced mistakes and increased my confidence before each hiking day.

Daily Hiking Routine Planning

Developing a structured daily routine helped me make the most of my time in the Lofoten Islands. I quickly learned that flexibility is important, but having a general plan for each day improves efficiency and reduces stress.

I usually started early in the morning to take advantage of stable weather conditions and quieter trails. Starting early also allowed me to adjust my schedule if unexpected delays occurred during the hike.

Breaks were planned strategically rather than randomly. I paid attention to energy levels and used rest periods to recover, hydrate, and assess route progress.

Evening planning was equally important. I reviewed the next day's route, checked weather updates, and prepared gear in advance. This reduced morning preparation time and helped me start each day smoothly.

This routine created a balance between structure and adaptability, which proved essential for multi-day hiking experiences.

Common Mistakes To Avoid

During my time exploring the Lofoten Islands, I observed and occasionally made mistakes that could easily have been avoided with better planning. One of the most common issues was underestimating trail difficulty.

I initially assumed that shorter distances meant easier hikes, but elevation gain and terrain conditions often made routes more challenging than expected. Learning to evaluate all factors together improved my decision making.

Another mistake was not checking weather conditions frequently enough. In a region where conditions can change quickly, relying on a single forecast is not enough. Regular updates became an essential part of my routine.

Overpacking was another issue I had to correct early on. Carrying unnecessary items increased fatigue without adding real benefit. I learned to prioritize functionality over quantity.

Avoiding these mistakes significantly improved both safety and enjoyment during my hiking experience.

Final Travel Tips For Lofoten Islands

By the end of my journey, I had gathered several practical insights that shaped how I would approach future trips. One of the most important lessons was to remain flexible at all times. Weather, trail conditions, and transportation schedules can change quickly, and adaptability is essential.

I also learned that slowing down enhances the experience. Instead of trying to cover as many locations as possible, spending more time in fewer areas allowed me to appreciate the landscape more deeply.

Another important tip is to respect both nature and local communities. The Lofoten Islands are not just a tourist destination but a living environment where people work and live. Awareness and respect improve the overall experience for everyone involved.

Finally, I realized that preparation and simplicity are key. A well-planned but lightweight approach leads to a more enjoyable and manageable hiking experience.

Closing Reflections And Personal Insights

Looking back on my time in the Lofoten Islands, I recognize that the experience was shaped as much by preparation and mindset as by the trails themselves. Every hike taught me something new about patience, awareness, and adaptability.

I came to understand that hiking in this region is not just about reaching viewpoints or completing routes. It is about engaging with an environment that is constantly changing and learning how to move within it responsibly.

The combination of dramatic landscapes, unpredictable weather, and cultural richness created an experience that went beyond expectations. Each challenge contributed to a deeper appreciation of the islands.

What stayed with me most was the balance between effort and reward. The more carefully I prepared, the more meaningful each hike became.

This final chapter represents the lessons I carried home with me. They continue to influence how I approach outdoor travel, reminding me that thoughtful preparation and respect for nature always lead to better experiences.

CONCLUSION

When I set out to explore the Lofoten Islands through hiking, I expected dramatic scenery, challenging trails, and unpredictable weather. What I did not fully anticipate was how deeply the experience would shape the way I approach travel, preparation, and time spent in nature. Looking back, I realize that this journey was not just about reaching summits or completing routes, but about learning how to move through a landscape that constantly demands awareness and respect.

Across the chapters of this guide, I shared what I learned from planning routes, managing gear, navigating changing conditions, and understanding the realities of multi-day trekking in an Arctic environment. Each experience added another layer of understanding. Simple decisions such as when to start a hike, what to carry, or where to rest became essential parts of a much larger system that determines safety and enjoyment in the outdoors.

One of the most important lessons I took from Lofoten is that preparation is never wasted effort. Careful planning gave me the freedom to adapt when conditions changed. It allowed me to enjoy moments that were unexpected without feeling unprepared or overwhelmed. In contrast, poor preparation tended to reduce options and increase stress, especially in remote areas where support is limited.

I also learned that nature in the Lofoten Islands does not follow convenience. Weather shifts quickly, terrain can be demanding even on short routes, and distance often feels longer than it appears on a map. Accepting this reality changed how I approached each hike. Instead of trying to control the experience, I focused on responding to it with patience and awareness.

Another lasting insight came from the balance between effort and reward. Some of the most memorable views required steady climbs, early starts, or long days on the trail. Yet those moments felt more meaningful precisely because of the effort involved. The landscapes were not simply seen; they were earned step by step.

Beyond the physical aspects of hiking, I also gained a deeper appreciation for responsible travel. Preserving fragile environments, respecting local communities, and minimizing impact are not optional considerations. They are part of what makes it possible for places like Lofoten to remain beautiful and accessible in the future.

As I reflect on the entire journey, I realize that the most valuable outcome was not a list of destinations completed, but a shift in mindset. I now approach outdoor travel with more patience, more preparation, and a stronger respect for natural environments and the people who live within them.

For anyone planning a hiking adventure in the Lofoten Islands, I would encourage more than just route planning. Pay attention to conditions, prepare thoroughly, stay flexible, and allow space for the unexpected. The islands will challenge you, but they will also reward you in ways that are difficult to put into words.

In the end, this guide is not only about hiking in Lofoten. It is about learning how to travel with intention, how to respect powerful natural environments, and how to find meaning in the journey itself rather than only the destination.

Made in the USA
Monee, IL
24 June 2026

55669441R00056